Lessons Learned: Critical Information Infrastructure Protection

How to protect
critical information infrastructure

Lessons Learned: Critical Information Infrastructure Protection

How to protect critical information infrastructure

TOOMAS VIIRA

IT Governance Publishing

Every possible effort has been made to ensure that the information contained in this book is accurate at the time of going to press, and the publisher and the author cannot accept responsibility for any errors or omissions, however caused. Any opinions expressed in this book are those of the author, not the publisher. Websites identified are for reference only, not endorsement, and any website visits are at the reader's own risk. No responsibility for loss or damage occasioned to any person acting, or refraining from action, as a result of the material in this publication can be accepted by the publisher or the author.

Apart from any fair dealing for the purposes of research or private study, or criticism or review, as permitted under the Copyright, Designs and Patents Act 1988, this publication may only be reproduced, stored or transmitted, in any form, or by any means, with the prior permission in writing of the publisher or, in the case of reprographic reproduction, in accordance with the terms of licences issued by the Copyright Licensing Agency. Enquiries concerning reproduction outside those terms should be sent to the publisher at the following address:

IT Governance Publishing
IT Governance Limited
Unit 3, Clive Court
Bartholomew's Walk
Cambridgeshire Business Park
Ely, Cambridgeshire
CB7 4EA
United Kingdom
www.itgovernance.co.uk

First published in the United Kingdom in 2018
by IT Governance Publishing.
ISBN 978-1-84928-957-3

ABOUT THE AUTHOR

Toomas Viira has worked in cyber security for more than 20 years. In 2004 he joined RIA (*www.ria.ee*) (Estonian information system authority), in 2005 he began activities to create CERT Estonia, and in 2007 he was a member of the team that protected Estonia from large scale cyber attacks. Viira is also one of the authors of the Estonian Cyber Security Strategy. In 2009 he was appointed head of the Critical Information Infrastructure Protection department in RIA. He managed several national critical information infrastructure (CII) projects such as CII mapping, CII risk analysis and CII operators' penetration tests, developing risk analysis and response plans for large-scale state-level emergencies, and more. He has the following certifications: CISSP, CISA, CISM, CRISC, ISO 27001 CIS LI, ITIL® Foundation and ITIL Service Strategy. Viira is the founder of *www.ciipunit.com*.

ACKNOWLEDGEMENTS

I would like to express my thanks to Heli Tiirmaa-Klaar, Jaak Tepandi, Janno Kase, Kaimar Karu, Rünno Reinu, Siim Aben, Maarten Souw, Giuseppe G. Zorzino and Christopher Wright, who read and reviewed the manuscript, providing very useful comments and feedback. I would like to extend a special thanks to Mari Seeba, who read every sentence and analysed the content of the manuscript with the utmost care.

I'd like to thank the IT Governance Publishing team and the members who worked on this book: Jonathan Todd, Luke Milner and especially Vicki Utting, who managed me through the full publishing process and gave me very useful guidance.

I would like to express my thanks to all the colleagues I have worked with over the years and with whom I have had the opportunity to make great things in the field of cyber security.

CONTENTS

Contents

INTRODUCTION

The way organisations operate and provide services has changed considerably over the past decades. Their capability to produce something has also grown significantly. This has become possible largely due to information technology solutions, which have become indispensable and a natural part of business. Those who try to manage without them achieve only limited performance and functionality. It often seems that doing things without IT solutions is plain impossible. Information plays an important role in management decisions and in business processes. IT solutions have allowed organisations to increase their efficiency in order to be competitive. However, do we even know and realise what happens when IT solutions are not working – when they simply don't function at all or not in the way we expect them to?

People and organisations consume electricity generated by various types of power plants: nuclear, hydroelectric, thermal, wind, solar and others. We consume the services of communications service providers, such as voice telephony and data communication. We cannot get by without transport service providers – we need companies that operate in aviation, marine transport or on railways. We need operational water supply companies to get water from the tap. Hospitals, clinics and ambulance crews must work to provide medical help to people. Financial service providers must be operational so we can withdraw money from ATMs or make bank transfers. Most of these companies use information systems to provide their services. It wouldn't be possible without them.

However, these systems must be very well protected against cyber attacks. Cyber attacks[1] could interrupt[2] all or part of critical infrastructure services for several hours or days, bringing health, safety, economical, environmental and reputational consequences[3].

Risks should also be minimised in terms of technological faults and human error. Are the systems that provide critical infrastructure services protected? How well are they protected? Considering today's threats and attack capabilities, it feels like many of these systems are not adequately protected.

Billions of people use the services of these companies, and this number is increasing rapidly. There are fewer and fewer places where people don't consume any services provided with the help of IT solutions.

But how is it possible that services consumed by so many people are provided using relatively vulnerable systems? In many instances, even the most basic security measures have not been implemented.

I have been working in the field of protecting CII since 2005 and organised the relevant activities in a country where the use of e-services and dependence on information technology

---

[1] A Stuxnet cyber attack on a steel mill caused damage to Germany's industrial infrastructure by destroying human machine interaction components: *www.sentryo.net/cyberattack-on-a-german-steel-mill*

[2] In December 2015 a successful cyber attack on a power grid in the Ukraine compromised information systems and disrupted electricity supplies to end consumers: *https://en.wikipedia.org/wiki/December_2015_Ukraine_power_grid_cyberattack*

[3] The NonPetya ransomware attack is estimated to have cost shipping giant Maersk $300m and forced it to halt operations at 76 port terminals around the world. They were just one of the companies affected globally: *www.theregister.co.uk/2017/08/16/notpetya_ransomware_attack_cost_us_300m_says_shipping_giant_maersk/*

is among the highest in the world. People often ask me the same questions: How is CII protected in Estonia and what have you learned?

The current weak protection of CII, the threats and attack capabilities lurking in cyberspace, and the questions people have asked prompted me to write this book. My goal is to help you be as successful as possible in protecting your CII, and do so as quickly and with as little effort as possible, irrespective of whether you work for a critical infrastructure service provider, a company that organises the provision of critical infrastructure services, a company that provides services to a provider of critical infrastructure or somewhere else.

The book is aimed at people who organise the protection of critical infrastructure, such as chief executive officers, business managers, risk managers, IT managers, information security managers, business continuity managers, and civil servants from ministerial level to analyst level. Most of the principles and recommendations I describe are also valid in organisations that are not critical infrastructure service providers.

There are several hyperlinks throughout the book. If you are reading the print version, please visit *www.ciipunit.com/lessonslearned* where you will find an online library for easier access to the links. On the same website, I have also provided links to several CII incident pages and CII audit checklists, and will regularly update the website with content related to the book.

PART 1: CRITICAL INFRASTRUCTURE

CHAPTER 1: CRITICAL INFRASTRUCTURE SERVICES

'The next Pearl Harbor we confront could very well be a cyber attack that cripples our power systems, our grid, our security systems, our financial systems, our governmental systems.'[4] – Leon Panetta

People have a variety of needs in their daily lives: water, food, clean air, a home and electricity. We also consume many other benefits such as transport services, communication services, television and radio programmes, medical services and banking services. Without some of them, we probably wouldn't survive – not for long, anyway. Some services are more important to different people at different times – transport connections, communications and medical services may be more or less essential, depending on your circumstances. A common understanding of primary needs is relatively easy to achieve, but when pinpointing vital services we may often end up with different opinions. Defining such services depends on geographic location, climate, season, people's way of life and other factors. There are services that people have become used to over decades, and their absence causes uncertainty or puts our security at risk. Mobile communication is a good example of this: it is important for people to be in contact with their loved ones, but 30 years ago we managed just fine without mobile phones. We've become increasingly used to them and our dependence on them has grown. Many of us feel like we can't live without social networks.

---

[4] *www.huffingtonpost.com/2011/06/13/panetta-cyberattack-next-pearl-harbor_n_875889.html*

The lines between vital, socially important and other services consumed by us cannot be clearly and unequivocally defined. From the viewpoint of protecting critical infrastructure, it is important that such services are defined and written down somewhere. Every country should have a specific law that regulates this field. Defining critical services is bound to lead to discussions and possibly arguments about whether or not a specific service is critical, or why one service is critical and another is not. Preparing the list of services is still in its early stages in terms of the entire process of protecting critical infrastructure and CII, and there is still a lot to do. The law can be amended if an important service was left out or a service that was deemed critical shouldn't actually be regarded as such.

These critical services must be operational:

- power supply
- oil and gas supply
- water supply and sewerage
- harbours
- rail traffic
- air traffic
- data telephony
- data communication
- settlements and cash withdrawals
- law enforcement
- medical assistance.

The list is not final, and the circumstances, characteristics and needs of each country should be taken into account.

Lesson 1: Define critical infrastructure services.

CHAPTER 2: DESCRIPTION OF SERVICE AND SERVICE LEVEL

'Critical infrastructure is vitally important to all of us because it provides the necessities: water and food; the electricity and gas; the telecommunications and broadcasting services that keep us in touch and help us to conduct our business; the health services that keep us alive; the banking and finance system that keeps our economy running; and the transport system that gets us – and the goods we need – from A to B.'[5] – George Brandis

Preparing the list of critical infrastructure services described in the previous chapter is the first step. However, the list alone is not enough for planning the activities that follow. It is also important to describe the critical infrastructure services. How and on what basis can we say that a critical infrastructure service is functioning? How do we know what a specific critical service is and what characterises it? If we don't know what a functioning service looks like, then it's impossible for us to objectively assess whether or not it is functioning. Does a service function as needed?

Every critical service should be described. The description of a critical infrastructure service should allow the service provider, consumers and other stakeholders to understand what can and cannot be expected from the specific service. All critical infrastructure services can be characterised with different criteria and parameters. The requirements for and

---

[5] *www.attorneygeneral.gov.au/Speeches/Pages/2014/Second%20Quarter%202014/6June2014-OpeningAddressOfTheCriticalInfrastructureResilienceConference.aspx*

service level of a critical infrastructure service should also be determined. Power coming from the grid always has the same tension and frequency, and we're used to this. It's possible that these parameters have been determined in regulations. Power supply companies enter into contracts with their clients. These contracts or the general conditions of services may also contain other aspects that describe the service and service level. They might contain the number to call in the event of faults, determine how quickly the company has to react to faults, how quickly faults have to be eliminated, etc. Sometimes they state the length of a power cut from which the client is not charged for the service. In these cases, we can say that a service level has been determined between the service provider and the client. However, the service level of a critical infrastructure service should be determined from the viewpoint of the state.

It's likely that there are many services that have not been adequately described and for which the necessary service level has not been determined. Or, if a service level has been determined, it was not done in consideration of the fact that the service is a critical infrastructure service and its consumers may have higher expectations regarding the continuous operation of the service.

These parameters should be determined for every critical infrastructure service:

- maximum tolerable downtime
- recovery time objective.

Maximum tolerable downtime is the downtime that an organisation, specific sector or country can tolerate. 'Maximum tolerable' can be defined at business, sector or country level and these could be different. A critical infrastructure service provider should follow the shortest defined downtime.

Recovery time objective is the defined time during which systems and services should be brought up and running.

Service-specific indicators that characterise the operating level of the service must be defined for the majority of services: a minimal quantity of calls in a mobile communications network, the quantity of banknotes withdrawn from an ATM in a certain unit of time, the guaranteed minimal water pressure at specific measurement points, the minimal number of passengers served by a harbour in a certain unit of time, etc.

The above is the so-called primary requirement in the process of building a critical infrastructure protection system. We should then think about the operational needs of critical services in the event of crises of different severity and define them if possible. What are the critical infrastructure services that should definitely work in the event of a crisis and at what level should they operate?

Lesson 2: Describe the critical infrastructure service and determine its service level.

CHAPTER 3: PROVIDERS OF CRITICAL INFRASTRUCTURE SERVICES

'Critical infrastructure is diverse and complex not only because of the variety of sectors it covers, from communications, emergency services, information technology to nuclear reactors and transportation systems; it is complex also due to the special nature of its ownership.'[6] – Dean Thompson

Once the list of critical infrastructure services has been prepared, they have all been described and their service levels determined, the next step is to identify the providers. Critical infrastructure service providers are not only public-sector organisations. In many countries, essential elements of critical infrastructure are owned and operated by private companies. Depending on the service, market, regulations and many other factors, a service may be provided by one or several service providers. Some countries may only have one provider of a certain service if the service provider is a monopoly, or only one service provider may have the right to provide a certain service in a certain region. The number of monopolies has decreased in the past 20 or 30 years. Many countries have opened their markets in the communication and energy sectors, which in the past were often controlled by monopolies.

In the case of a monopoly when there is only one service provider on the market, this service provider must be

---

[6] *https://ro.usembassy.gov/remarks-by-u-s-charge-daffaires-ad-interim-dean-thompson-at-the-critical-infrastructure-protection-forum/*

considered the critical infrastructure service provider.

What happens when there is more than one service provider on the market? Many other factors should be considered, such as the number of clients to whom the service is provided, market share, production volume and capacity, number of clients in a certain geographic region, etc.

Which service providers will be considered critical infrastructure service providers and which ones will not? Depending on the sector, services and possible criteria for defining critical infrastructure services, as well as reaching the relevant agreements, identifying these service providers may take a lot of time.

For example, if there are many voice telephony service providers, which of them should be considered critical infrastructure service providers? There may also be situations where some providers only operate in a certain geographic region and don't provide their service nationwide. Some of these service providers may have the biggest market share in a specific region and not provide their services in another. This means that geography must be considered when defining the criteria for a critical infrastructure service provider.

Possible criteria for qualifying an organisation as a critical infrastructure services provider:

- Number of clients nationwide.
- Number of clients in a certain region.
- Number of people living in a certain administrative district.
- Market share of the service provider according to turnover.

- Production volume, capacity, etc.
- Number of service points in the country or a certain administrative district.
- Client or clients to whom the service is provided (e.g. a communications operator that provides services to other critical infrastructure service providers).
- A service provider of transnational importance (e.g. a critical infrastructure service provider in the EU – an operator that provides a service to a significant number of clients abroad).
- An operator that provides international connections, etc.

The list of critical infrastructure providers should be reviewed and updated at least annually or after essential changes.

Lesson 3: Define the providers of critical infrastructure services.

CHAPTER 4: CRITICAL ACTIVITIES AND REQUIRED RESOURCES

'Despite the fact that cyber-attacks occur with greater frequency and intensity around the world, many either go unreported or are under-reported, leaving the public with a false sense of security about the threat they pose and the lives and property they impact.'[7] – Daniel Wagner

In order to provide a critical infrastructure service reliably, it is necessary to know how the service is provided. What kind of business processes must be operating so that the service provider can provide the service and the consumer can consume it? Providing critical infrastructure services often depends on various sub-services without which the service cannot be provided. Depending on the organisation and the service, such services may be provided internally: one department provides a service to another department. The other option is to outsource services from external providers. If the provision of services is organised internally, then the parties and business processes connected to the critical infrastructure service must be identified inside the company. In such cases, it is usually easier to understand which business processes are necessary to provide the critical infrastructure service, which resources are needed, what the connections between the different resources are like and how the whole system works.

However, the services consumed for service provision are

---

[7] *www.huffingtonpost.com/daniel-wagner/the-growing-threat-of-cyb_b_10114374.html*

often not all internal and the services of external providers are also needed. Critical infrastructure service providers often have several external service providers. They in turn often rely on subcontractors. There are many cases where a critical infrastructure service provider doesn't even know how long a certain supply chain is and who they actually depend on. Not to mention knowing the ability of a specific company to provide a specific service or sub-service, their capability in the event of a crisis, the background of the specific company, etc.

It is important to know what is needed to provide every critical infrastructure service at the required service level. What kind of business processes guarantee that the service is operational and which business processes are essential? In general, the business processes needed to provide critical infrastructure services can be divided into three categories:

- Business processes without which the service cannot be provided.

- Business processes that are necessary for providing the service, but the service can for some time be provided without such business processes being operational (possibly at reduced functionality and/or load).

- Business processes that do not have a significant role in the provision of the service, that is, the service can be provided without these processes being operational.

There are many companies where the processes needed to provide critical infrastructure services have not been described, there is no understanding of the connections between processes, and the operation of various processes is not measured. Sometimes the bigger the company, the more difficult the processes are to describe. However, as a company grows in size, it needs to give more attention to describing its processes and their efficiency.

The resources needed for different processes should be identified after the processes have been listed and described. The following questions should be asked:

- Who is responsible for operating each process?
- How is the smooth operation of processes guaranteed?
- What happens if there are faults or disruptions?
- What is the impact of disruptions on providing the main service?

It should also be clear whether the preconditions needed for providing a critical service at the required service level have even been created, whether the service levels of outsourced services have been agreed with subcontractors and whether the service levels have been agreed inside the organisation of the critical infrastructure service provider. Would all the above even make it possible to provide the service at the required level or should changes be made?

Lesson 4: Identify the critical activities, resources and responsible persons needed to provide the critical infrastructure service.

CHAPTER 5: INTERDEPENDENCIES OF SERVICES

'By better understanding and quantifying the consequences, both economic and societal, of a severe cyber hazard on our country's critical infrastructure, we underline the level of responsibility amongst each of the key stakeholders in this value chain. Through hyper-connectivity, we have created fantastic opportunities for smarter infrastructure use that also bring with them a complex set of cyber risks for the foreseeable future.'[8]
– Simon Ruffle

In the previous chapter, we determined that providing critical infrastructure services needs several business processes and took a look at this from the viewpoint of a critical infrastructure service provider. However, the big picture should also be analysed in terms of the functioning of the state. It is obvious that many critical infrastructure services depend on one another, on many other services that are not regarded as critical infrastructure services, and on power supply. In most countries, many critical infrastructure services also depend on the operation of services in the ICT sector, such as voice telephony, data communication or information systems. There are also

---

[8] www.quicken.com/investing/stock-quotes/LMT/Lockheed-Martin-Corp/Collaboration-on-Critical-National-Infrastructure-Cybersecurity-Key-to-Minimising-UK-Economic-Risk-According-to-New-Study/600-201604120803PR_NEWS_USPRX____CL68540-1

other critical infrastructure services and sectors that are connected and depend on one another:

- You need a working mobile phone or landline to call emergency services.
- Operational radio communication is necessary for organising police and ambulance crews.
- Police cars and ambulances need fuel, so we need working petrol stations.
- Card payment terminals need to work so that the fuel can be paid for.
- These terminals need a working banking information system and data communication network.
- A data communication network needs electricity to work.
- Eliminating electrical failures needs working telephone communications.
- An operating security company is needed to guarantee the physical security of sites.
- Sending alarm signals from sites needs a working data/voice telephony network.
- A boiler house needs gas (or the supply of a different type of fuel) to work.
- A water supply company needs electricity to work.
- Air traffic control needs various working information systems and a working connection with other air traffic control centres as well as between control centres and aircraft.
- Airfields depend on good maintenance of runways, working runway lights, security checks of passengers and baggage, aircraft fuelling and maintenance, etc.

- Communications networks need electricity and operational network components: telephone exchanges, network nodes, mobile communication masts, routers, communications channels, servers of different communications networks that provide specific services, settlement systems, software, etc.
- Power can be supplied when electricity generation, transmission networks and distribution networks are all working.

This list could go on and on as it does not list all the possible dependencies of a service.

As said above, most services need a power supply to function. We cannot get by without it. Or if we can, then for only a very short time. Organisations may have diesel generators, but they must be refilled with fuel. How big are the generators' fuel tanks? Can extra fuel be obtained from somewhere during a power cut? Can a petrol station give fuel from its tanks when there is no electricity?

The above demonstrates rather well that while most services depend on electricity and communications, they also depend on many other services and this makes the whole situation more complicated.

From a state perspective, a strong overview of dependencies is vital. If such an overview doesn't exist, it becomes very difficult to assess the scale and impact of different types of incidents. Every responsible ministry should have oversight of their governance area and draw up a list of state-level dependencies. At the country level, governments should appoint an agency to be responsible for emergency management. The same agency should have information on the dependencies in all critical infrastructure sectors, cross-sectoral dependencies and cross-border dependencies.

Heavily CII-dependent states have more complex interdependencies and will need information systems to run almost everything. This means power supply becomes more important because information systems are bricks without electricity.

Lesson 5: Analyse and identify the interdependencies of services and their reliance upon power supplies.

CHAPTER 6: VISUALISATION OF INFORMATION

'The greatest value of a picture is when it forces us to notice what we never expected to see.'[9] – John Tukey

After implementing everything described in the previous chapters, we should have a list of critical services, descriptions of the services and service providers, and an analysis of the interdependence of services at a certain level. This has generated a lot of information that must be managed, changed or updated if necessary. A proper overview of it should also be created.

This can be done with a word processor, spreadsheet or database, but they are not the best methods as finding the data and getting a good overview of it in these formats will be difficult or even impossible.

It would be better to visualise this information somehow, which will reveal the connections that otherwise only a good data analyst could find. While it might be simpler for people who deal with the topic every day to understand these connections, this information must be comprehensible to people who do not, especially those who will be responsible for protecting critical infrastructure.

Data visualisation could be the solution to the aforementioned problems. Data visualisation is important at the levels of companies, sectors and the entire state. At the level of companies, it should support describing the company's business processes, creating connections

---

[9] Tukey, John W. (1977). Exploratory Data Analysis. Pearson. ISBN 978-0201076165

between them, resource planning and much more.

Visualisation at the level of the state and sectors gives a good overview of which critical or non-critical infrastructure services are needed to provide a specific critical infrastructure service. What kind of service providers are needed and where are they located?

Visualising the things that were described in previous chapters also makes many other activities easier. It helps us prepare risk analyses when the interconnections and dependencies of services have to be analysed. It can be used in impact analyses when it's necessary to assess whether and how the interruption of a service affects other services.

Visualisation tools can also help with various training programmes. 'Performing' different scenarios using the relevant solutions is an excellent approach. What happens when we 'break' this connection or this site in the visualisation application? How quickly will something happen and what impact will it have?

The necessity and usefulness of visualisation tools in clarifying and selling CII activities to organisations should not be underestimated. People are often surprised when they see how much critical infrastructure services depend on other services and the extent to which they are connected to one another. They are also surprised when they realise that a critical infrastructure service depends on ICT at all or that the critical infrastructure service is also interrupted when the ICT service stops working.

<u>Lesson 6</u>: Visualise critical infrastructure data.

PART 2: CRITICAL INFORMATION INFRASTRUCTURE

CHAPTER 7: IDENTIFICATION OF IMPORTANT INFORMATION SYSTEMS

'An unidentifiable asset is the same as a non-existent one (look hard to identify your assets).'[10] – Dave Logan

The first chapter results in a list of critical infrastructure services, the second chapter helps create a description of critical infrastructure services, the third chapter is the basis for setting the criteria needed to determine critical infrastructure service providers, the fourth chapter should result in an analysis of what it takes to provide critical infrastructure services, the fifth chapter will help identify the interconnections of critical infrastructure services, and the sixth chapter will give us a clear, visualised picture of critical infrastructure.

Based on the above, most critical infrastructure services have characteristics or peculiarities that differentiate them from one another. The services differ in how they are provided and what is needed to provide them. There may be critical infrastructure services among them that are provided without any use of information systems, or if they are used, then only for supporting activities. This means activities that don't have a direct impact on the provision of the service. On the other hand, there are critical infrastructure services where the provision of the service stops either immediately or sometime after information systems stop working. There may be critical infrastructure services that can continue at

---

[10] *www.slideshare.net/dyohn/dl-yohn-notes-quotes-from-asp-02-25-10*

reduced capacity and/or functionality when information systems stop working.

We regard systems that are necessary for providing critical infrastructure services as important information systems. To find these information systems, we need to know how the critical infrastructure service is provided. Defining important information systems is easier in organisations where business processes have been described and it is clear which services are provided by the IT department. Organisations need to understand how a service is provided: what is needed to provide the service, the responsibilities of different business entities, the inputs and outputs of different activities, etc. It is important to differentiate processes that are directly needed to provide a critical infrastructure service, whether it's producing a certain item or providing a service.

Defining important information systems is also complicated when external IT service providers provide the critical infrastructure service in addition to your 'own' IT services. IT services provided externally may be very different, such as hosting services, network administration, software development, managed security services, workstation management, etc.

External service providers may also use subcontractors to provide their services, which complicates the service provision process further in terms of understanding it and understanding the extent to which various parties participate in providing the service.

Once the information systems have been identified, we need to assess their importance in providing the critical infrastructure service. A three-level importance scale could be used, as it is relatively simple:

1. The information system is essential for providing the critical infrastructure service, as the service stops either immediately or a very short time after the information system stops working.
2. The information system is necessary for providing the critical infrastructure service, but the service can be provided at reduced functionality and/or capacity without the information system. There are workarounds for when the information system stops working.
3. The information system is not important for providing the critical infrastructure service as the service does not depend directly on it. Information systems are used for many supporting business processes of critical infrastructure services, for example, accounting, human resources management, etc.

Using such a scale should give a good overview of the information systems needed to provide a critical infrastructure service and their importance. When a service is provided by external service providers, the importance of their information systems should also be assessed.

ICT is a critical sector in many countries. However, depending on the country, information systems play a significant role in most sectors and consequently in providing critical services. This means that critical information systems are not only used in ICT but also in energy, transport, finance, medicine and many other sectors.

Lesson 7: Identify important information systems and assess their importance.

CHAPTER 8: INTERDEPENDENCIES OF INFORMATION SYSTEMS

'If we are to take full advantage of new technology to drive economic growth, we also need to fully understand and manage the risks.

One of the great difficulties of dealing with cyber security is the complexity of the landscape.

This is caused in part by the huge variance in the types of perpetrators attacking us, the harm they want to cause and the targets they choose to focus on.'[11] – John Key

We analysed the interdependencies of critical infrastructure services in chapters four and five. Now that we have identified the information systems necessary to provide critical infrastructure services, we need to analyse how they are connected and dependent on one another.

Finding and mapping interconnections at the level of information systems is much more difficult and time-consuming than at the level of critical infrastructure services because the systems and the connections between them are considerably more complex. Critical infrastructure services can be viewed from an abstracted perspective and this simplifies what you need to know. Information systems must be looked at from a more granular and precise perspective, because the architecture complexity level

---

[11] *www.beehive.govt.nz/speech/speech-cyber-security-summit*

within them is much higher. Data used for one business process could go through several information systems managed by an organisation's IT department or by an external IT service provider, data may be hosted in the Cloud, etc.

As our scope contains information systems necessary for critical infrastructure services, we should also give attention to the industrial control systems used to provide several extremely important critical infrastructure services. Communications systems should also be considered. Communications solutions, which a few years ago were more like a group of their own, have quickly integrated into general IT solutions and the same technological solutions are often used, for example, an IP network and the same IT solutions.

It must be ascertained which information systems are necessary in certain parts of the business process. The previous chapter showed us the level of importance of each information system. But we have to go into more detail now. Every critical infrastructure information system should be 'taken apart' to understand whether it depends on other information systems, which ones and how. In simpler cases, it may be just one application located in a specific server, which in turn is located in a specific server room. This makes analysis easier. However, there are still several circumstances that must be considered when such cases are analysed, such as where the users of the application are located. Even this one information system can only function if there is an operating data communications network between the users and the information system's server, and that the security of the application is guaranteed with firewalls, virus protection, intrusion detection systems and other tools. It's also important that the infrastructure services of the server room are working: power supply, cooling, fire extinguishers and other supporting services and systems.

Often, the situation is not so simple. Let's look at an energy company's distribution network. Energy companies usually have thousands of substations across the country, or in the region or regions of the country where the service is provided. There are thousands of controllers in these thousands of substations. These controllers are usually monitored and controlled from somewhere in the company's control centre. This needs a data communications network between the centre and the substations. There are usually many commutators, routers, modems, etc. in the data communications network, as well as radio link equipment if radio links are used to access the substations in different geographic locations. Then there are firewalls and intrusion detection systems to guarantee security.

One of the first major challenges for the energy company is to carry out an inventory of the devices in the (IP) network and, even more importantly, keep it up to date and revise it once a quarter or once a month. In some cases, it should be revised even more frequently. An inventory data update should also be made after changes in the network that may impact operations. Software should be used to carry out an inventory. Once an inventory has been completed, the connections between different components should be analysed. Which components are connected to one another and how do different components affect one another?

The services provided by external partners should not be forgotten when the relevant analysis is done. It is necessary to consider who external IT service providers depend on. Do they in turn outsource services from someone else and which other infrastructure services do they depend on?

<u>Lesson 8</u>: Identify and analyse the interconnections and dependencies of information systems.

CHAPTER 9: FOCUSING AND PRIORITISATION

'It is only a matter of the "when," not the "if" that we are going to see something dramatic.' [12] – Michael Rogers

The way a country categorises its critical national infrastructure into sectors varies considerably from country to country [13]. The categories often include energy, health and transport to name just a few. The dependence on information systems varies according to the sector and the critical infrastructure service. The dependence on information systems by different service providers is also different.

From the critical infrastructure service provider's perspective, an organisation may provide several services and only some of them are considered critical infrastructure services. A good example of this is banks, which often have relatively large service portfolios. Cash withdrawal and payments are usually considered critical services. Many other services they provide, such as loans and leasing, investment, insurance and safety deposit boxes, are not considered critical.

However, there can also be service providers that only offer critical infrastructure services and nothing else, such as water suppliers and heat producers.

It is important for critical infrastructure service providers that the service levels of all services are determined and that

---

[12] www.nsa.gov/news-features/speeches-testimonies/testimonies/adm-rogers-testimony-20nov2014.shtml
[13] https://publicwiki-01.fraunhofer.de/CIPedia/index.php/Critical_Infrastructure_Sector#cite_note-1

37

the resources needed to provide them without disruptions have been allocated. The requirements arising from regulations must also be considered when service levels are determined.

From the state's perspective, the most important thing is to determine critical infrastructure services. However, even when they have already been listed, there are still services that are more important than others. Which critical infrastructure services are very important, which are important and which are less important? It may not be easy to determine, but it should still be done. We could try dividing the services into categories of importance.

To a certain extent, critical infrastructure services should be categorised according to which services might be needed in various stages of a crisis. Depending on the country, crises of different levels could be defined from the ordinary situation up to martial law. There could be two, three, four or more levels of crisis. Irrespective of the number of levels, it would be good to know which critical infrastructure services work in various crisis situations and at which levels they should do it.

It is also necessary to define the critical infrastructure services that significantly depend on information systems. Persons dealing with cyber security issues should focus on protecting these services as they cannot work when information systems are down.

Focusing and prioritising should therefore be done at the following:

- The level of critical infrastructure services.
- The level to which a critical infrastructure service depends on IT.

- The level of providers of specific critical infrastructure services.

- Upon setting priorities and allocating resources internally in the critical infrastructure service providers.

As the resources of the state and critical infrastructure service providers are limited, it is particularly important to allocate resources to protect important services and systems.

People who deal with cyber security should not be dealing with critical infrastructure that does not depend on IT. Priorities should be set for critical infrastructure that depends on IT according to the extent of dependence, possible risks and the scale of the impact of any disruptions in providing the critical infrastructure service.

<u>Lesson 9</u>: Focus on more critical services and prioritise your activities.

PART 3: THREATS, VULNERABILITIES, RISKS, IMPACTS

CHAPTER 10: THREATS AND VULNERABILITIES OF INFORMATION SYSTEMS

'An aggressor nation or extremist group could gain control of critical switches and derail passenger trains, or trains loaded with lethal chemicals. They could contaminate the water supply in major cities, or shut down the power grid across large parts of the country.'[14] – Leon Panetta

As a result of the activities described in the seventh and eighth chapters, we should know which information assets are necessary for critical infrastructure services and what the connections are between these assets. Their level of criticality from the position of providing critical infrastructure services should also be assessed.

Next, we should identify the threats to the provision of critical infrastructure services. A threat is something that has the potential to damage the assets needed to provide various services. Vulnerability is related to assets and allows a threat to damage them. A threat may be caused by people (intentionally or unintentionally) or nature, and can arise from inside or outside an organisation. An intentionally caused threat may target a specific organisation or its information assets.

Organisations that provide critical infrastructure services should focus on the threats that may disrupt those services. Completed lists of threats can be found in different standards

---

[14] *www.nytimes.com/2012/10/12/world/panetta-warns-of-dire-threat-of-cyberattack.html*
www.telegraph.co.uk/news/worldnews/northamerica/usa/9604794/US-at-risk-of-cyber-Pearl-Harbor-Leon-Panetta-warns.html

and frameworks. It is important to keep the list of threats short at first and focus on the main threats, at least until the risk assessment process has been completed. Otherwise, the discussion may focus for a long time on topics that may not be that important at all.

Cyber threats have changed considerably in recent years. The increasing use of IT systems and new technological solutions for providing services is making critical infrastructure service providers more vulnerable, and many new attack vectors have emerged. The spread of malware is increasing, cyber attacks are more professional, cyber crime is growing, different groups and some states are creating and strengthening their cyber attack capabilities, and the organisers behind cyber attacks are still difficult to apprehend. These developments have also created a fertile ground for attacks against critical infrastructure organisations.

Disruptions resulting in power cuts are a good example of this. Natural events, such as storms, are one of the causes of power cuts, but power cuts may also be caused by intentional or unintentional activities. Vandalism at a power substation is an intentional action but a human error by an employee at the energy company's control centre is an unintentional action. The vandalism may be regarded as a targeted attack if the person who committed it or ordered it wanted to attack that specific substation or a consumer who receives electricity from that substation.

If a threat takes advantage of the vulnerability of information assets, it may cause loss of the availability, confidentiality or integrity of those assets. In some cases, several of these components may be lost at the same time, or the loss of one may cause the loss of another.

Confidentiality is lost when an unauthorised person gets access to an organisation's data (e.g. an unauthorised person gaining access to the configuration of an industrial control system). Integrity is lost when an unauthorised person changes the data (e.g. when an unauthorised person changes the configuration of an industrial control system). And availability is lost when an authorised person can't access the data or service when it is needed (e.g. an unauthorised person blocks access to the configuration of an industrial control system).

The principle of moving from the general to the detailed should be the basis for identifying threats and vulnerabilities. This principle could be used to identify the threats and vulnerabilities pertaining to critical infrastructure service providers, different sectors and the entire state.

<u>Lesson 10</u>: Identify threats and vulnerabilities.

CHAPTER 11: ASSESSMENT OF THE IMPACT OF SERVICE DISRUPTIONS

'The World Economic Forum affirmed that in the next 10 years there is a 10% likelihood of a major Critical Information Infrastructure breakdown with possible economic damages of over $250 billion. Incidents and attacks are on the rise.

The big message was that cybersecurity is a matter that cannot be left to the technical people. It is a matter for board levels. '[15] – Neelie Kroes

As mentioned earlier, not all critical infrastructure services are the same. Some are more important than others, such as power supply and communication services that are needed to operate other critical infrastructure services. Then there are services that depend less on other services and can work relatively independently. Some services are more important at certain times than others, and some are more important for some people than others.

What happens when, for whatever reason, a critical infrastructure service does not work for one minute, ten minutes, one hour, ten hours, one day or ten days? What is the impact of the disruption? Will it immediately result in a threat to people's lives and health, will it cause economic damage, is there a risk of environmental pollution, is there a threat to the service provider's assets or to the assets of users?

---

[15] *http://europa.eu/rapid/press-release_SPEECH-13-51_en.htm*

These impacts should be assessed on different scales. They can be the life and health of people, economic, environmental or reputation-related. The size of the area affected by the service disruption should also be considered when impact is assessed, as well as the number of the service provider's clients and service users that would be affected by the service disruption.

Impact assessment and analysis is a lot easier if the connections between the services have been described. It is even easier when data has been visualised.

The whole critical infrastructure service may not be disrupted in all incidents. A disruption may simply lower service quality, or it may be possible to provide the service at reduced capacity or reduced functionality. It is important to analyse in terms of the duration of a disruption whether and how quickly damage will increase.

Does the disruption of a service influence the operation of another service, and how? A disruption in power supply is highly likely to influence all other critical infrastructure services. Many companies use an uninterruptible power supply and generators to guarantee power supply for their systems. Generators can usually guarantee power supply in the event of power cuts for a couple of hours, depending on the size of the generator's fuel tank. However, it would be necessary to put more fuel in the generator's tank during longer power cuts, so where would you get the extra fuel from if the power cut affects a whole region or an even bigger area? If no fuel is available, the generator is only a temporary solution.

Uninterruptible power supply and electricity generators also guarantee that server rooms and data centres work. However, even if there is electricity in a data centre, there might not be at the bank or an ATM, which means that the client cannot use their services. Even if an uninterruptible power supply or generator was used at the bank, it might still not be enough. Data communication would still be down, as there would be no electricity in some of the data network hubs.

The impact of the disruption of services on the provided critical infrastructure service must also be considered in an impact assessment. How will the disruption of another critical infrastructure service affect the provided service?

Analysing the impact of incidents and the extent of the damage they may cause will hopefully give a better understanding of possible risks and how much should be invested in cyber security.

Lesson 11: Assess the impact of service disruptions.

CHAPTER 12: RISK ASSESSMENT

'More and more devices and machines are now connected to the Internet, along with more and more areas of our lives and productive activities. Extensive risk analyses are required in order to properly assess the dangers and minimise the probability of their occurrence.'[16] – Michael Hange

After analysing the threats and vulnerabilities affecting information assets, we should assess the risks associated with IT services. What kinds of incidents can affect the work of the information systems that support critical infrastructure services? What kinds of incidents are certain to disrupt service provision? Analysing possible incidents is time-consuming but necessary. Using a power cut as an example again, we should 'act out' the scenarios that could cause a disruption in the service:

- Power cut caused by the organisation.
- Power cut caused by factors outside the organisation.
- Power cut that started due to factors outside the organisation, which was also caused by a mistake inside the organisation.

Existing security measures should be assessed to see whether and how much they already help reduce risks. If the server room of a critical infrastructure service provider only receives power from one substation, then this is a risk that should be dealt with. However, if the server room receives

---

[16] *www.bsi.bund.de/SharedDocs/Downloads/EN/BSI/Publications/Magazin/BSI-Magazin_2015.pdf*

power from two substations, the probability of a disruption is somewhat smaller. If a critical infrastructure service provider has two server rooms at different locations, the probability of a power cut that affects IT services is smaller still.

Statistics on incidents that have occurred and their analysis will give a specific input of what has already happened. When the causes of incidents are analysed, it should lead to an understanding of why they have occurred. Have any conclusions been drawn from the incidents and have additional security measures been applied to prevent new incidents? It is also necessary to keep an eye on the surrounding environment for technological changes, new vulnerabilities, the attack vectors used, incidents taking place in other organisations in the same sector, etc.

Most critical infrastructure service providers don't have the capacity to carry out a detailed risk analysis of their information systems. It would simply require too many resources and cost too much. A high-level risk assessment could be the starting point. Once the first results have been achieved with this methodology, the next step could be an assessment of risks at a more detailed level.

The people who prepare sector-based risk analyses should collect the risk analyses of the critical infrastructure service providers operating in the sector and create summaries from them.

Those who prepare risk analyses to the extent of the entire state should proceed from sector-based risk analyses and make summaries of them.

However, it is likely that something important may go unnoticed or that there are circumstances that don't get enough attention. Often, companies prepare risk analyses primarily from their own (the company's) point of view and look at the scenarios that they think are likely and may threaten their business activities. The scenarios that the company finds too unlikely or that there is nothing it can do anyway are therefore not given any attention. Things that may not be problems for a company may be a very serious problem for the state. The state should therefore have central competence that reviews the risk analysis prepared for the state and makes the required amendments. If necessary, the level of the specific company will be viewed again to get more information for preparing the risk analysis, etc.

Lesson 12: **Assess the risks associated with the service and information system.**

PART 4: PROTECTION ACTIVITIES

CHAPTER 13: IMPLEMENTATION
OF SECURITY MEASURES

'The CEO must make it clear that security is not just an IT problem – it is a priority for the business that is top of mind. Business and technology leadership must work together to discuss potential risks and find solutions that protect intellectual property and financials alike.'[17] – John Chambers

One of the results of a risk assessment should be distinguishing risks of different levels. The easiest way is to use a three-level scale to assess risks (high, medium, low). Whether and how the level of each risk could be reduced should also be assessed. One option is to implement extra security measures.

Not many extra security measures should emerge if a high-level risk assessment method was used. However, if the critical infrastructure service provider has used a detailed risk assessment method, hundreds of extra security measures may appear to be necessary. The resource-intensive detailed risk assessment method may be necessary in some specific, narrow areas, but most likely not for the whole organisation. An alternative solution would be to use baseline security methods, which help achieve considerable results faster if skilfully implemented.

Considering the complexity of today's information systems, protecting the whole company's information systems and the

---

[17] www.forbes.com/sites/frontline/2015/07/13/why-cybersecurity-leadership-must-start-at-the-top/print/

associated environment needs considerable effort and many security measures.

Which security measures should they be and where can they be obtained? Who should decide which security measures to apply and at which level?

Here are three options in the context of CII:

1. The critical infrastructure service provider decides which security measures it applies to protect the information systems needed by the critical infrastructure service. The state does not establish any rules regarding the guarantee of cyber security.
   The critical infrastructure service provider should consider the service levels described above and agreed on between the relevant parties. They must also be considered in guaranteeing the availability, integrity and confidentiality of information systems.

2. The state advises setting a standard as the basis for protecting the relevant information systems. Compliance with this standard is not mandatory and it is not made mandatory with any regulations.

3. The state establishes some mandatory standards. These should be the minimum standards that critical infrastructure service providers must meet. The critical service provider must also decide whether and which standards it will use, and which extra security measures it will implement to guarantee the security of information systems and the associated environment.

Depending on the state, all the above options might be used. One option suits one state, whereas another may be better for a different country. The success of any particular system will depend on a range of factors, especially including how the entire system is structured.

A plan to implement security measures should be created at the level of the company after a cyber security standard has been chosen. Some measures will be important and can be quickly applied, whereas other important measures need more planning, expertise and resources. Someone should be appointed to implement each security measure and the status of the implementation should be checked at intervals.

Lesson 13: **Implement the necessary security measures.**

CHAPTER 14: ORGANISATION REQUIRED TO PROTECT CRITICAL INFORMATION INFRASTRUCTURE

'Governments here have a huge challenge. They need to find a model to protect their cyberspace in a situation where 80% of it does not belong to the government.' [18] – Heli Tiirmaa-Klaar

A well-functioning organisation is needed to launch activities to protect critical information infrastructure and keep them going. Every country should have an agency or agencies that coordinate and organise activities to protect critical infrastructure and CII. Regulations may often not specify the roles and functions of agencies, but legislation is very important. In order to launch the relevant activities, there should be an act or acts that list critical infrastructure services, the functions of critical infrastructure service providers, and the functions of the agencies that organise the provision of critical infrastructure services. The same act or sector-specific acts should determine the criteria for deciding which agencies are critical infrastructure service providers. Managing activities may be concentrated in one or several agencies. If activities are organised from several agencies, it is extremely important to determine the roles, functions and responsibilities of the different parties.

Activities concerning the cyber security of critical infrastructure are often concentrated in the cyber security units or departments of countries. They often include units

---

[18] *www.iiss.org/en/events/gsr/sections/global-strategic-review-2010-946c/sixth-plenary-session-6e03/heli-tiirmaa-klaar-0e22*

that deal with cyber security incidents, such as computer emergency response teams (CERTs). Cyber security departments often also deal with prevention, raising awareness, research and development, or organising or coordinating all of the above. They also support the ministries that deal with policy-making. Preparing and writing the cyber security strategy could be led from the ministry, but it should be supported by the divisions responsible for different areas.

There should be an institution in every sector that monitors the sector, including whether and how critical infrastructure service providers guarantee the provision of the services and their reliability. The agency that organises critical infrastructure services in every sector must be capable of assessing the risk analyses and business continuity plans prepared by every critical infrastructure service provider. If the agency doesn't have the necessary competence in an area, it should use relevant experts. Assessing the risks of information systems and cyber security is complicated and help from the state's cyber security department or experts should be sought. The agencies that organise the provision of critical infrastructure services often can't and even don't need to have the relevant experts and in-depth knowledge.

Every critical infrastructure service provider must create the relevant structure in its organisation that would create the premises for guaranteeing the security, including cyber security, of the critical infrastructure services at the level of the organisation. The management of every organisation that provides critical infrastructure services must understand the risks that may threaten the provision of the critical infrastructure service. Management should appoint the person responsible for cyber security in the organisation and organising activities in the relevant area. An organisation that depends largely on IT should hire an information security manager or outsource the relevant service. The information security manager role should be separate from the IT department.

The information security manager and the IT department should assess the level of protection of information systems and, if necessary, develop extra security measures. The information security manager should prepare a plan for applying security measures and a relevant overview for the CEO, which includes the resources needed.

Management should allocate the resources necessary to assure information security, and should emphasise the importance of information security in the organisation and every employee's responsibility in guaranteeing it.

There is no universal model that suits all countries; there is no universal model that suits all sectors; there is no universal model that suits all service providers. You must instead create the organisation, determine the roles and responsibilities of the parties, and monitor the system to make sure that it is working.

Lesson 14: Create a functioning organisation to protect critical information infrastructure.

CHAPTER 15: NIS DIRECTIVE

'There are only two types of companies: those that have been hacked, and those that will be.'[19] – Robert Mueller

Critical infrastructure service providers must follow several regulations. In the EU, critical infrastructure service providers must comply with both EU legislation and legislation imposed at the national level. EU laws are imposed, generally, through one of two models: directives and regulations. Regulations apply directly and need not be adopted by the member states to take effect, while directives instruct the member states to create domestic legislation to put the directive into effect.

CII service providers should be aware of the Network and Information Systems (NIS) Directive (Directive (EU) 2016/1148 of 6 July 2016 concerning measures for a high common level of security of network and information systems across the Union). By 9 May 2018, EU member states must adopt and publish the laws and administrative provisions necessary to comply with this directive.

The NIS Directive is the EU's attempt to raise overall cyber security levels among infrastructure service providers in the EU and promote cooperation between member states. The Directive regulates CII service providers in the energy, transport, banking, financial market infrastructures, health,

---

[19] *https://archives.fbi.gov/archives/news/speeches/combating-threats-in-the-cyber-world-outsmarting-terrorists-hackers-and-spies*

drinking water supply and distribution, and digital infrastructure sectors.

Article 14 of the Directive defines the requirements for security and for incident notification as they apply to operators of essential services. To slightly paraphrase:

- Take appropriate and proportionate technical and organisational measures to manage the risks posed to the security of network and information systems which they use in their operations.

- Take appropriate measures to prevent and minimise the impact of incidents affecting the security of the network and information systems used for the provision of such essential services, with a view to ensuring the continuity of those services.

- Notify, without undue delay, the competent authority or the CSIRT (Computer security incident response team) of incidents having a significant impact on the continuity of the essential services they provide.

Each member state has to impose these within national regulations. There are probably already several member states whose regulations include most or part of the requirements.

The Directive also sets obligations for member states' national competent authorities, single points of contact and CSIRTs. Depending on the country, these functions can be fulfilled by one or more organisations. Several countries have created cyber security agencies that carry out all the functions.

According to the Directive, each member state:

- Shall adopt a national strategy on the security of network and information systems defining the strategic objectives and appropriate policy and regulatory measures with a view to achieving and maintaining a high level of security of network and information systems (Article 7, clause 1).

- Shall designate one or more national competent authorities on the security of network and information systems ('competent authority') (Article 8, clause 1).

- Shall designate a national single point of contact on the security of network and information systems ('single point of contact') (Article 8, clause 3).

- Shall designate one or more CSIRTs (Article 9, clause 1).

- Shall establish a list of the services [essential for maintaining critical societal and/or economic activities] (Article 5, clause 3).

Annex I of the Directive describes the requirements and tasks of CSIRTs:

- CSIRTs ensure a high level of availability of their communications services.

- CSIRTs' premises and the supporting information systems shall be located in secure sites.

- CSIRTs shall be equipped with an appropriate system for managing and routing requests, in order to facilitate handovers.

- CSIRTs shall be adequately staffed to ensure availability at all times.

- CSIRTs shall rely on an infrastructure the continuity of which is ensured. To that end, redundant systems and backup working space shall be available.

According to Article 15 of the Directive, the national competent authority should have the powers and means to require operators of essential services to provide:

- The information necessary to assess the security of their network and information systems, including documented security policies.

- Evidence of the effective implementation of security policies, such as the results of a security audit carried out by the competent authority or a qualified auditor and, in the latter case, to make the results thereof, including the underlying evidence, available to the competent authority.

Since the Directive is relatively general in wording, it is necessary to develop several specific instructions and find a common methodology for consistent application.

Lesson 15: Follow regulations to improve cyber resilience of critical infrastructure services.

CHAPTER 16: ASSESSMENT OF THE SECURITY LEVEL

'If you're not doing scans and penetration tests, then just know that someone else is. And they don't work for you.'[20] – George Grachis

Can we be certain that our information systems are protected? Are the information systems used to provide critical infrastructure services adequately protected, especially considering the expertise and capabilities of those who might organise cyber attacks?

People often say that their systems are well protected, because nothing has ever happened. Does the fact that nothing has happened really mean they are well protected? Or is it a case of it just hasn't happened yet? To establish the answer an organisation might use a self-assessment to gauge the security of its information systems. The organisation's internal audit function could then give its opinion of the security of information systems. The organisation should also order an external audit to receive an independent opinion; internal audit departments often don't have the competence required for auditing information systems, and are unlikely to have auditors with the skills to audit the security level of automatic control systems.

When ordering audits of information systems, the auditor should hold the certificate of an information systems auditor (e.g. CISA, ISO 27001 Lead Auditor). Certified auditors should include the relevant specialists in their work, whether

---

[20] *www.cyberrescue.co.uk/library/quotes*

they are industrial control system security experts, IP network security experts, application level security experts, etc. Audits should not remain solely at the level of giving an opinion of the information security policies of the CII provider, but should include actual testing that gives answers about the real level of security.

Attention must be paid to the reliability of the service provider, and background checks of all the auditors and experts who perform the work must be carried out. Since many critical infrastructure service providers are private companies, they should cooperate with the relevant public authorities that can advise on suitable service auditors and experts.

Requiring experience in carrying out similar audits is a good idea. The potential impact on the systems that will be tested must also be considered, as even the smallest attack test that looks harmless at first may impact operating systems.

An audit report is prepared following an audit. The report should include the findings made during the audit and recommendations for their elimination. The auditors and testers should also prepare a summary presentation of the audit results, which the organisation's management should most definitely attend.

Management should be interested in the auditors' opinion of the security level of the information systems used to provide the critical infrastructure service. They must also know whether and how many different vulnerabilities were found, how they can be eliminated, and how much money, expertise and time this would take.

The audit should highlight the money, expertise and time an attacker would need to organise an attack. Auditors may also point out risks and/or weaknesses related to non-human actors or non-malicious incidents from insiders, which can also be detrimental to the security of information systems. Such figures can make management think and act more. They can provide a very simple illustration of how low the level of security is in some organisations, or even reveal there is no security in the organisation, or parts of it, at all.

The security of information systems used to provide CII should be regularly audited to obtain objective opinions.

Lesson 16: **Assess the security level of your information systems yourself and ask external experts to assess them as well.**

CHAPTER 17: NETWORK SCANNING

'Security vulnerabilities have been found in all types of webcams, cameras of all sorts, implanted medical devices, cars, and even smart toilets – not to mention yachts, ATM machines, industrial control systems and military drones.

All of these things have long been hackable.'[21] –
Bruce Schneier

When we discuss the security of critical infrastructure, people often say that their systems are secure because they are not connected to the Internet. They presume that this is both true and that they are therefore secure from all threats to their information systems.

However, search engines to find Internet-connected devices have been developed and implemented in recent years, and often find devices that you might not expect to need Internet connectivity. Different devices can be found by entering certain keywords in the relevant search engines. To complete searches more successfully, the user can enter specific keywords contained in the web interface banners of devices. Search engines also allow the user to specify a country, city, IP range, operating system, port, etc. as search criteria. Various filtering options make it possible to find very exciting things on the Internet.

What isn't connected to the Internet nowadays? Skilful searches can find the air conditioning control systems of

---

[21] *www.schneier.com/blog/archives/2013/08/hacking_consume.html*

buildings, heating control systems, lift control systems, smart home appliances, medical equipment, security systems, boiler house systems, power station systems, water supply systems and much more.

Many of these systems that can be found on the Internet are protected with default passwords or passwords that are easy to figure out. Some systems need no authentication at all or allow you to try various passwords an infinite number of times.

When someone believes their systems should not be accessible from the Internet, they should make sure they really are inaccessible. People dealing with the information security of CII should therefore use different tools to determine whether their organisation's systems can be found on the Internet. Security managers should know or find out the keywords used in the web interface banners of the organisation's systems. They should use various search engines to find devices that are possibly connected to the Internet. External security experts should also be asked to search for the organisation's systems.

If the searches reveal that systems that shouldn't be accessible from the Internet are actually accessible, they should be disconnected from the Internet as soon as possible. When networks really need to be connected for some reason, the traffic between them, and the traffic between the networks and the wider Internet, should be strictly restricted and the risks associated with this explained to the persons involved.

When attackers gain access to the ICS network, they don't need many skills to disturb or disrupt a system. Since it's often impossible to add security to industrial control systems or to configure them to be more secure, the majority of security measures must be implemented at network level.

Lesson 17: **Scan networks yourself and ask external experts to scan them as well to find the organisation's systems that shouldn't be connected to the Internet, but still are connected.**

CHAPTER 18: BUSINESS CONTINUITY PLAN AND TESTING

'The best way to get management excited about a disaster plan is to burn down the building across the street.'[22] – Dan Erwin

All critical infrastructure service providers should be prepared for worst-case scenarios. Serious preparation begins with doing the things the organisation can do itself, such as creating a business continuity plan that sets out the actions taken in the case of various incidents. Worst-case scenarios could include a fire, flood, earthquake, act of vandalism or a cyber attack. Cyber attacks should be differentiated by type and target in a business continuity plan because the activities needed for business continuity and recovery are different for different types of attacks. If risk analyses have been prepared, they are an input during the preparation of a business continuity plan.

An information system disaster recovery plan should also be prepared. How should people act when an information system stops working, and what should be done to recover it? How are working information systems guaranteed? Who sends failure notices? Who reacts to them and how quickly? Which action is taken? How are different parties informed?

Business continuity and disaster recovery plans should be regularly tested. Plans that look good on paper are not much use if it's unknown whether they would actually work.

---

[22] *https://infosecphils.wordpress.com/infosec-quotes/*

There are several ways to test a business continuity plan. Table-top testing is the most reasonable and cheapest option: people gather at a table and an emergency is simulated in the course of testing. The scenario for primary testing could be one that carries the biggest risk and causes the most damage, or one that is easy to organise to make the participants understand how the relevant exercises work. The purpose of these exercises is to assess whether everyone understands the plan and their role and duties, whether there is information exchange and how it works, whether the necessary resources have been identified and are available, whether there are any faults in the plan, whether goals will be reached, whether changes should be made in the plan and whether extra training should be given.

While a table-top exercise is usually the most reasonable option for starting the testing process, the test that is the most realistic and probably the most expensive is causing an actual disruption. For some critical infrastructure service providers, of course, carrying out such a test is out of the question and impossible. The critical infrastructure service may be interrupted in full or in part during such testing. A part of the service or the provision of the whole service in a certain region may be suspended. The focus can be only on testing IT systems. For example, critical infrastructure service providers that use two server rooms can interrupt the functioning of one of the server rooms and then check whether the systems will work (or stay working) from the second server room. Such testing needs thorough and careful preparation to avoid causing real damage to the operating systems and clients, but they give the best understanding of the situation. It is important to assess the results of the tests, draw conclusions and make the necessary changes to the business continuity plan.

There has been a movement towards sectoral, national and international cyber training in recent years. Participating in such training is good for critical infrastructure service providers because they don't have to contribute to its preparation. It also gives their employees experience that can be implemented in organising cyber security and help guarantee the continuity of services.

Business continuity and disaster recovery plans should also be prepared at the state level, which help prepare for the interruption of critical infrastructure services and coordinate recovery.

Lesson 18: Prepare business continuity and disaster recovery plans and test them at reasonable intervals.

PART 5: PROTECTION SYSTEM SUPPORTING ACTIVITIES

CHAPTER 19: RELIABLE RELATIONS AND MAINTAINING THEM

'Pulling a good network together takes effort, sincerity and time.' – Alan Collins[23]

Knowing people and the communication channels between them is very important for cyber security. When a crisis occurs, there is no time to start identifying the people who deal with this, looking for their contact details and contacting them: contacts and reliable relations must be established beforehand because the information related to cyber security is often sensitive.

It is necessary to know people from inside the organisation as well as people from other organisations. They can be from the public or private sectors, IT specialists or people from other walks of life, senior managers, from the same country or abroad.

All have a role in the activities aimed at protecting critical infrastructure and CII, which can be successful when communication works well.

When the state defines, describes and agrees on critical services and determines their service levels, these are also largely based on good cooperation between people in the public and private sectors.

People in private sector organisations may be used to the relations between the service provider and the regulator, or communicating with the tax authority. However,

---

[23] www.pinterest.com/pin/417920040400575538/

communication initiated in relation to risk, especially IT risk assessment, may come as a surprise to private sector organisations in many countries. Such interest from the state is usually a positive surprise for critical infrastructure service providers.

Critical infrastructure service providers should have the contact information of the relevant authorities and their employees who can help handle cyber incidents, such as CERTs. National CERTs communicate with the CERTS of other countries when, for example, finding a solution for a specific cyber incident.

The people who deal with cyber security should know one another and have one another's contact details across various channels, so that they can be contacted even when some communications networks are not working.

Organising joint events, such as training, seminars and information days, helps maintain good relations and promotes information exchange. Building a good cooperation network takes months, if not years.

Lesson 19: Establish reliable relations and maintain them.

CHAPTER 20: SHARING INFORMATION

'It is abundantly clear to anyone working in cyber security that no-one has anything like complete visibility of the problem. Cyberspace is simply too vast for any organisation – public or private sector – to have sight on everything that's going on.'[24] –
Francis Maude

The importance of incident-related information cannot be underestimated in organising cyber security activities and handling cyber incidents. Relevant and correct information that is sent and received in time can often have a deciding role in preventing cyber security incidents and protecting against cyber attacks.

When a network of people dealing with cyber security has been established in a country, it has taken the first step towards a working information exchange. As we said in the previous chapter, having reliable relations in this network is important, as is knowing the right people and having their contact details.

It is necessary to agree on the principles of information exchange, which must cover the kind of information that is communicated as well as when, to whom and how. In countries that have established CERTS, it is usual for the CERTs to send information about the vulnerabilities they have detected to their communities and give advice on how to act securely. CERTs have become information exchange

---

[24] www.gov.uk/government/speeches/cyber-security-information-sharing-programme

centres in many countries.

For example, when a critical infrastructure service provider suffers a cyber attack, they should send information about it to the country's CERT. Depending on the type of the attack, the CERT helps the critical infrastructure service provider if necessary, sends information about the attack in an anonymised format to those that could be attacked in a similar manner, and recommends how to prepare for the cyber attack and what to do if they are attacked.

Some countries have also established sector-specific units that deal with cyber security. They may be called the sector's CERTs or given different names. The principle should stay the same – the critical infrastructure service providers that should benefit from the information should also receive it.

Cyber attackers exchange information very well. They have no obstacles in sharing information – no state borders or legal restrictions. Reaching a rapid, coordinated and reliable level of information exchange often takes public authorities and countries a long time.

Attention should also be given to marking information when it is communicated. Using the traffic light protocol is common when information about protecting critical infrastructure is shared. Marking the created document in red, yellow, green or white tells the people who handle the documents how to act with the relevant information.

Information is often classified as a state secret of some level, which becomes an obstacle to its communication. Even if a critical infrastructure service provider needs information about possible cyber attacks, it may not get it. A public authority does not communicate the relevant information because the employee of the critical infrastructure service provider who should receive the relevant information does not have a permit for accessing state secrets or the permit's level is not high enough. This is where countries need to find suitable solutions, either by lowering the security class of the specific documents, or the critical infrastructure service provider employees who deal with security issues need to apply for the necessary permits.

To guarantee cyber security, it is necessary to exchange information inside the sector, between sectors, inside a country and between countries.

Lesson 20: Share information and be a part of networks where information is shared.

CHAPTER 21: TRAINING PEOPLE

'When it comes to security, people matter as much as software and hardware, if not more. A fortress may have thick and strong walls, but will still be vulnerable to attack if the guards carelessly leave the gate open. Similarly, careless or ignorant employees can severely weaken a business' defence against cyber threats. '[25] – Yaacob Ibrahim

Without competent and motivated people, starting, carrying out and completing activities in the area of protecting the entire CII is very difficult.

Competent people are needed at all levels, from the strategic level to the cyber security specialists.

Developing the strategy of activities aimed at protecting critical infrastructure should start from the people who work for public authorities and are responsible for the relevant area. While developing the strategy for protecting critical infrastructure is a significant challenge, developing one for protecting critical information infrastructure is at least as significant. It may be worth developing this strategy as a component part of a larger cyber security strategy in order to define context and boundaries.

The organisations that provide critical infrastructure services should also employ people who understand cyber security and the relevant risks. People often don't realise how much critical infrastructure services depend on IT services, and

---

[25] *www.csa.gov.sg/news/speeches/speech-at-nsc-2015*

they don't know or don't believe that a cyber attack can disturb or disrupt the provision of a critical infrastructure service.

It may seem incredible to some politicians, high-ranking officials or business managers that cyber attacks can disrupt electricity generation or the transmission network.

It is therefore important to train the relevant people and raise their awareness of the dependence of critical infrastructure services on IT systems, existing threats, cyber protection capabilities and the damage that cyber attacks can cause.

The role of managers of organisations that provide critical infrastructure services is also important because they can emphasise the importance of the topic. Their decisions often determine how much resource is allocated for the activities. In the case of businesses, decisions about major investments also depend on the owners of the companies. When management's understanding of the importance of the topic is poor, they may not allocate the necessary resources for cyber security. Managers and owners of companies should therefore be educated about cyber threats, the ways in which cyber attacks are carried out and their impact. The duties of the CEO in arranging information security activities should also be ascertained.

The information security manager of an organisation also has an important role, as they are responsible for launching and maintaining an information security management system (ISMS).

In fact, every employee has a role in guaranteeing cyber security. Their awareness of cyber threats must be raised and they should be taught how to act in certain situations to help them perform their roles.

Training people and raising their awareness should be a constant process. Organisations should prepare a programme, which would help plan the necessary activities and allocate the resources needed. If any significant changes occur in cyber threats or methods of attack, these topics should be added to the training plans.

Lesson 21: Train people to make sure they are aware of cyber threats and know how to behave.

PART 6: PERFECTING THE SYSTEM

CHAPTER 22: IMPROVEMENT OF THE SYSTEM

'When it is obvious that the goals cannot be reached, don't adjust the goals, adjust the action steps.'[26] – Confucius

The purpose of creating and maintaining a CII protection system is to protect what is vitally important. The things that are important for citizens, companies and public authorities must be protected, as should the way we live and do things.

Changes must be made if the protection system does not work the way it should. Problems can be found by assessing at intervals which activities are successful and which are not, which areas' goals have been achieved, and which areas' goals have not been achieved but progress has been made. There may be areas where no progress has been made for a long time or progress is very slow, so the reasons why must be analysed and necessary changes made.

The workings of the different parts of the system should be assessed at intervals. All critical infrastructure service providers should assess activities from the viewpoint of their organisation. Organisations that organise and regulate the provision of critical infrastructure services at the sectoral level should analyse this provision in the sector and ascertain how reliable and protected it is. The risk analyses and business continuity plans of critical infrastructure service providers should be assessed. Incidents must be analysed to

---

[26] *www.brainyquote.com/quotes/authors/c/confucius.html#pzgm5wtCh4Oj2OuU.99*

identify their causes and how they were solved.

The agency or agencies that coordinate and organise activities to protect critical infrastructure and CII at the national level should assess how the system works. Measurable results should be set as the goal when activities are planned.

When the goals set in strategies are achieved, the situation should be reassessed and new goals set. When the goals set in strategies were not achieved, the plans for implementing them should be assessed. A great deal goes into the relevant protection system, and even more must be contributed to make that system successful. Furthermore, every country and every sector has its unique features, and there is no universal model for protecting critical information infrastructure.

Lesson 22: If the CII protection system does not work as planned and does not give the desired output, make improvements to the system.

PART 7: BACKUP PLAN

CHAPTER 23: LIFE WITHOUT IT

'Everything is being run by computers. Everything is reliant on these computers working. We have become very reliant on Internet, on basic things like electricity, obviously, on computers working. And this really is something which creates completely new problems for us. We must have some way of continuing to work even if computers fail.

So preparedness means that we can do stuff even when the things we take for granted aren't there. It's actually very basic stuff – thinking about continuity, thinking about backups, thinking about the things that actually matter. '[27] – Mikko Hypponen

I get up in the morning and turn the radio on: all I hear is static. I change the station, but it's just more static. I turn on the TV: there is no picture or sound. I open my laptop to read the news online, but there is no Internet connection. I want to pay by card at the café, but the terminal is not working. I drive to work: there are massive queues on the roads because no traffic lights are working. I want to call work, but my phone cannot find the network. I get to the office and want to open the door with my access card, but the card reader is not working. I go back to the street and walk to the subway station. The streets are full of people: it turns out that the trains are not running. The timetables at the station have gone blank. I leave the subway and manage to get a cab. I ask the driver to take me to the airport. I want to pay the fare by card,

---

[27] www.ted.com/talks/mikko_hypponen_fighting_viruses_defending_the_net/transcript?language=en

but the card terminal in the cab is not working either. I give the driver my last banknotes. There are more people than usual at the airport. I take my place in the check-in queue, but then there is an announcement that check-in cannot be completed because the computer systems are down. We're not told when they will be fixed. All the information boards at the airport are blank. Perplexed people stand in the queue and wait. Arriving passengers are not allowed through passport control, because the information systems are not working. The lights on all runways are off. I leave the airport and walk to the supermarket. There is a lot of noise and commotion. Card terminals are still not working. Many people are angry because they have goods in their baskets and trolleys, but they cannot pay for them. Some people try to get past the checkouts without paying. Some are eating and drinking the groceries in their trolleys. I go to the toilet next to the store. I want to flush, but there is no water. I want to wash my hands, but there is no water. I find some coins in my pocket and rent a bike to cycle back to the city. I see massive traffic jams as I ride the bike. There is a police patrol on a corner and I ask them what's going on. The police officers tell me they don't know. They cannot contact the station, because their radios are not working. I keep riding on. There is a hospital on the way. There is a noisy crowd in front of its entrance and security guards are trying to prevent people from entering the hospital. It appears that some people were not allowed to see a doctor because the hospital's information systems are down and the hospital couldn't look up medical records or confirm insurance. They were sent away because emergency care is all that is provided. I carry on cycling towards the city and suddenly I smell something awful. I ride on and see wastewater flowing down the street. At first, I think that it's a localised problem:

a broken pipe or something. I ride on for a few kilometres and see the next spot where wastewater is flowing onto the street. It seems to be part of a bigger problem. The city's wastewater pumps are not working.

This could go on and on...

Something like this could happen if our IT systems stopped working or stopped working the way they should. Could critical infrastructure service providers provide their services without IT systems? At what level and to what extent? Would it be possible to reduce dependence on IT systems, how much would it cost, who would pay and who determines the level to which dependence should be reduced? Have critical infrastructure service providers practised providing their services without IT systems?

<u>Lesson 23:</u>

Be prepared to provide critical infrastructure services without IT systems.

If possible, reduce dependence on IT systems.

If possible, during a crisis, provide critical services at reduced functionality and/or in reduced volumes.

'Back to the Stone Age. No, it's even worse than that. We don't know how to live like Stone Age people. Learning it would take a long time. Going (back) there would take a long time. Getting there would demand many human victims and cause a lot of damage.' – Toomas Viira[28]

---

[28] www.ciipunit.com/lessonslearned

APPENDIX 1: LESSONS LEARNED

Lesson 1: Define critical infrastructure services.

Lesson 2: Describe the critical infrastructure service and determine its service level.

Lesson 3: Define the providers of critical infrastructure services.

Lesson 4: Identify the critical activities, resources and responsible persons needed to provide the critical infrastructure service.

Lesson 5: Analyse and identify the interdependencies of services from the viewpoint of the state's operation.

Lesson 6: Visualise critical infrastructure data.

Lesson 7: Identify important information systems and assess their importance.

Lesson 8: Identify and analyse the interconnections and dependencies of information systems.

Lesson 9: Focus on more critical services and prioritise your activities.

Lesson 10: Identify threats and vulnerabilities.

Lesson 11: Assess the impact of service disruptions.

Lesson 12: Assess the risks associated with the service and information system.

Lesson 13: Implement the necessary security measures.

Lesson 14: Create a functioning organisation to protect critical information infrastructure.

Lesson 15: Follow regulations to improve cyber resilience of critical infrastructure services.

Lesson 16: Assess the security level of your information systems yourself and ask external experts to assess them as well.

Lesson 17: Scan networks yourself and ask external experts to scan them as well to find the organisation's systems that shouldn't be connected to the internet, but still are connected.

Lesson 18: Prepare business continuity and disaster recovery plans and test them at reasonable intervals.

Lesson 19: Establish reliable relations and maintain them.

Lesson 20: Share information and be a part of networks where information is shared.

Lesson 21: Train people to make sure they are aware of cyber threats and know how to behave.

Lesson 22: If the CII protection system does not work as planned and does not give the desired output, make improvements to the system.

Lesson 23:

Be prepared to provide critical infrastructure services without IT systems.

If possible, reduce dependence on IT systems.

If possible, during a crisis, provide critical services at reduced functionality and/or in reduced volumes.

ITG RESOURCES

IT Governance Ltd sources, creates and delivers products and services to meet the real-world, evolving IT governance needs of today's organisations, directors, managers and practitioners.

The ITG website (*www.itgovernance.co.uk*) is the international one-stop-shop for corporate and IT governance information, advice, guidance, books, tools, training and consultancy.

Publishing Services

IT Governance Publishing (ITGP) is the world's leading IT-GRC publishing imprint that is wholly owned by IT Governance Ltd.

With books and tools covering all IT governance, risk and compliance frameworks, we are the publisher of choice for authors and distributors alike, producing unique and practical publications of the highest quality, in the latest formats available, which readers will find invaluable.

www.itgovernancepublishing.co.uk is the website dedicated to ITGP. Other titles published by ITGP that may be of interest include:

- Information Security: A Practical Guide

  www.itgovernance.co.uk/shop/product/information-security-a-practical-guide-bridging-the-gap-between-it-and-management

- Build a Security Culture:

  www.itgovernance.co.uk/shop/product/build-a-security-culture

- The Case for ISO27001: 2013

  www.itgovernance.co.uk/shop/product/the-case-for-iso-27001-2013-second-edition

We also offer a range of toolkits that provide organisations with comprehensive and customisable documents to help create the specific documentation required to properly implement management systems or standards. Written by experienced practitioners and based on the latest best practice, ITGP toolkits can save months of work for organisations working toward compliance with a given standard.

Of particular interest to readers of this guide will be the ISO 27001 ISMS Documentation Toolkit:

www.itgovernance.co.uk/shop/product/iso-27001-iso27001-isms-documentation-toolkit

To see the full range of toolkits visit

www.itgovernance.co.uk/shop/category/itgp-toolkits

Books and tools published by IT Governance Publishing (ITGP) are available from all business booksellers and the following websites:

www.itgovernance.eu   *www.itgovernanceusa.com*

www.itgovernance.asia   *www.itgovernancesa.co.za*

Training Services

Organisations that are serious about their cyber security should employ best-practice security practices. Staff training is an essential component of the best-practice information security triad of people, processes and technology. IT Governance's ISO 27001 Learning Pathway provides information security courses from Foundation to Advanced level, with qualifications awarded by IBITGQ.

Many courses are available in Live Online as well as classroom formats, so delegates can learn and achieve essential career progression from the comfort of their own homes and offices.

For information on any of our courses, including PCI DSS compliance, business continuity, IT governance, service management and professional certification courses, please see: *www.itgovernance.co.uk/training.aspx.*

Professional Services and Consultancy

The confidentiality, integrity and availability of information is an important aspect of cyber security. Fortunately, an ISMS can be implemented as part of an information security management system (ISMS).

ISO 27001, the international standard for information security management, sets out the requirements of an ISMS, a holistic approach to information security that encompasses people, process, and technology.

Implementing, maintaining and continually improving an ISMS can be a daunting task. Fortunately, IT Governance's consultants offer a comprehensive range of flexible, practical support packages to help organisations of any size, sector or location to implement an ISMS and achieve certification to ISO 27001.

For general information about our consultancy services, including for ISO 27001, Cyber Essentials, ISO 20000, ISO 22301, C the PCI DSS, the GDPR and more, please see:

www.itgovernance.co.uk/consulting.aspx.

Daily Sentinel newsletter

You can stay up to date with the latest developments across the whole spectrum of IT governance subject matter including risk management, information security, ITIL and IT service management, project governance, compliance, and so much more by subscribing to our newsletter.

Simply visit our subscription centre and select your preferences:

www.itgovernance.co.uk/daily-sentinel

EU for product safety is Stephen Evans, The Mill Enterprise Hub, Stagreenan, Drogheda, Co. Louth, A92 CD3D, Ireland. (servicecentre@itgovernance.eu)

www.ingramcontent.com/pod-product-compliance
Lightning Source LLC
Chambersburg PA
CBHW070838070326
40690CB00009B/1605